Unleash Your Creativity with Knitting

Easy Projects Book for Teens

Chris A Haven

THIS BOOK BELONGS TO

The Library of

....

....

Did you like my book? I pondered it severely before releasing this book. Although the response has been overwhelming, it is always pleasing to see, read or hear a new comment. Thank you for reading this and I would love to hear your honest opinion about it. Furthermore, many people are searching for a unique book, and your feedback will help me gather the right books for my reading audience.

Thanks!

Table of Contents

SUMMARY

The Joyful Journey of Creating through Knitting: The Joyful Journey of Creating through Knitting is a deeply fulfilling and rewarding experience that allows individuals to express their creativity, while also providing a sense of relaxation and mindfulness. Knitting, an ancient craft that has been passed down through generations, offers a unique opportunity to create beautiful and functional items using just a pair of needles and some yarn.

One of the most remarkable aspects of knitting is the versatility it offers. From cozy scarves and hats to intricate sweaters and blankets, the possibilities are endless. With each stitch, the knitter has the power to transform a simple strand of yarn into a work of art. The process of selecting the perfect yarn, choosing a pattern, and watching the project come to life is truly magical.

Beyond the tangible results, knitting also provides numerous mental and emotional benefits. Many knitters describe the act of knitting as a form of meditation, allowing them to enter a state of flow and focus. The repetitive motions of knitting can be soothing and calming, reducing stress and anxiety. In a world filled with constant distractions and technology, knitting offers a much-needed respite and a chance to disconnect from the outside world.

Furthermore, knitting fosters a sense of accomplishment and pride. Completing a knitting project, whether it's a simple dishcloth or a complex lace shawl, brings a sense of satisfaction and fulfillment. The process of overcoming challenges, learning new techniques, and seeing the finished product is incredibly empowering. Knitters often find themselves inspired to take on more ambitious projects, constantly pushing their boundaries and expanding their skills.

In addition to personal fulfillment, knitting also provides an opportunity for connection and community. Knitting circles, also known as stitch and bitch groups, have become increasingly popular as a way for knitters to come together, share their projects, and offer support and encouragement. These gatherings create a sense of camaraderie and friendship, allowing knitters to connect with others who share their passion.

Moreover, knitting is a sustainable and eco-friendly craft. By choosing natural fibers and locally sourced yarns, knitters can reduce their carbon footprint and support ethical and sustainable practices. Additionally, knitting allows for the repurposing and upcycling of materials, reducing waste and promoting a more conscious approach to consumption.

In conclusion, the joyful journey of creating through knitting is a multifaceted experience that combines creativity, relaxation, mindfulness, and community. It offers a unique opportunity to express oneself, while also providing numerous mental and emotional benefits. Knitting is not just a hobby,

Using This Book to Become a Confident, Creative Knitter of Knitting:

If you have always been fascinated by the art of knitting and have been wanting to learn how to knit, then look no further than this book. This comprehensive guide is designed to help you become a confident and creative knitter, regardless of your skill level or previous experience.

The book starts off by introducing you to the basics of knitting, including the different types of knitting needles, yarns, and other essential tools.

It provides step-by-step instructions on how to cast on, knit, purl, and bind off, ensuring that you have a solid foundation to build upon.

Once you have mastered the basics, the book takes you on a journey through various knitting techniques and stitches. From simple garter stitch to more complex lace patterns, you will learn how to create beautiful and intricate designs with ease. Each technique is explained in detail, with clear instructions and accompanying illustrations to help you visualize the process.

But this book is not just about teaching you how to follow patterns and replicate existing designs. It also encourages you to unleash your creativity and experiment with different colors, textures, and patterns. It provides guidance on how to choose the right yarns for your projects, how to combine different stitches to create unique textures, and how to incorporate colorwork into your knitting.

In addition to the technical aspects of knitting, this book also delves into the artistic side of the craft. It explores the principles of design, such as balance, proportion, and harmony, and shows you how to apply them to your knitting projects. Whether you want to create a cozy sweater, a stylish scarf, or a decorative blanket, you will learn how to make thoughtful design choices that enhance the overall aesthetic of your work.

Furthermore, this book goes beyond just teaching you how to knit. It also provides valuable tips and tricks for troubleshooting common knitting problems, such as dropped stitches, uneven tension, and fixing mistakes. It offers advice on how to care for your knitted items to ensure their longevity and provides suggestions for joining knitting communities and participating in knitting events to further enhance your skills and connect with fellow knitters.

By the time you finish reading this book and working through the various projects and exercises, you will have gained the knowledge and confidence to tackle any knitting project with ease. Whether you want to knit for yourself, create handmade gifts for loved ones, or even start your own knitting business, this book will equip you with the skills and inspiration you need.

Exploring the Tools and Materials of Knitting: When it comes to knitting, there are a variety of tools and materials that are essential for any knitter. These tools and materials not only help in creating beautiful and intricate designs, but also make the knitting process much easier and enjoyable.

One of the most important tools in knitting is the knitting needles. These come in various sizes and materials, such as metal, wood, or plastic. The size of the needles determines the gauge or tension of the knitted fabric. Thicker needles create a looser fabric, while thinner needles create a tighter fabric. Knitting needles also come in different lengths, with shorter needles used for smaller projects like socks or hats, and longer needles used for larger projects like blankets or sweaters.

Another essential tool in knitting is the crochet hook. While primarily used for crochet, a crochet hook can also be handy in knitting for tasks like picking up dropped stitches or creating decorative stitches. Crochet hooks come in different sizes, just like knitting needles, and are made from various materials.

Yarn is the main material used in knitting, and it comes in a wide range of colors, textures, and fibers. The type of yarn you choose depends on the project you are working on and your personal preferences. Common types of yarn include wool, cotton, acrylic, and blends of different fibers. Each type of yarn has its own unique characteristics, such as warmth, softness, or durability.

In addition to knitting needles and yarn, there are several other tools that can be helpful in the knitting process. Stitch markers are small rings or clips that are placed on the knitting needles to mark specific stitches or sections of a pattern. These markers help in keeping track of the pattern and prevent mistakes. Tapestry needles are used for weaving in loose ends of yarn and sewing pieces of a knitted project together. Row counters are small devices that can be attached to the knitting needles to keep track of the number of rows or pattern repeats.

Other tools that can be useful in knitting include knitting gauges, which are small rulers with holes of different sizes to measure the gauge of a knitted fabric. Cable needles are used for creating intricate cable patterns, while stitch holders are used to hold stitches temporarily when working on other parts of a project.

Overall, exploring the tools and materials of knitting is an exciting journey for any knitter. With the right tools and materials, you can create beautiful and unique knitted items while enjoying the process of knitting.

Learning the Basic Stitches and Techniques of Knitting: Learning the basic stitches and techniques of knitting is an essential step for anyone interested in this timeless craft. Knitting is not only a creative outlet but also a practical skill that allows you to create beautiful and functional items such as scarves, hats, sweaters, and blankets.

Whether you are a complete beginner or have some experience with knitting, mastering the basic stitches and techniques will provide you with a solid foundation to build upon and explore more complex patterns and designs.

One of the first stitches you will learn when starting to knit is the knit stitch. This stitch forms the basis of most knitting projects and is relatively easy to master. To knit, you will need a pair of knitting needles and a ball of yarn. Begin by casting on, which is the process of creating the first row of stitches on your needle. There are various methods for casting on, such as the long-tail cast on or the knitted cast on. Once you have cast on, you can start knitting by inserting one needle into the first stitch on the other needle, wrapping the yarn around the needle, and pulling it through the stitch. Repeat this process for each stitch on the needle until you have completed a row. Then, turn your work and continue knitting in the same manner.

Another important stitch to learn is the purl stitch. The purl stitch creates a different texture and appearance compared to the knit stitch and is often used in combination with it to create various patterns and designs. To purl, you will follow a similar process as knitting but with a slight variation. Instead of inserting the needle from left to right, you will insert it from right to left. Wrap the yarn around the needle and pull it through the stitch, creating a loop on the right-hand needle. Repeat this process for each stitch on the needle until you have completed a row. Turning your work and alternating between knitting and purling will allow you to create different stitch patterns, such as stockinette stitch or ribbing.

In addition to the basic knit and purl stitches, there are other techniques that you will encounter as you progress in your knitting journey. One such technique is increasing, which involves adding stitches to your work to create shaping or to widen your project. Common methods of increasing include knitting or purling into the front and back of a stitch, or using yarn overs to create eyelets. Decreasing, on the other hand, involves removing stitches from your work to create shaping or to narrow your project.

Understanding Knitting Patterns and Instructions: Understanding knitting patterns and instructions is essential for anyone who wants to embark on a knitting project. Knitting patterns are like roadmaps that guide you through the process of creating a knitted item, whether it's a sweater, a hat, or a scarf. They provide you with the necessary information on the type of yarn to use, the size of the needles, and the specific stitches and techniques required to complete the project.

To fully comprehend knitting patterns, it's important to familiarize yourself with the various abbreviations and symbols commonly used in the knitting world. These abbreviations represent different stitches and techniques, such as knit (K), purl (P), yarn over (YO), and slip stitch (SL). By understanding these abbreviations, you'll be able to decipher the instructions and follow along with ease.

Additionally, knitting patterns often include charts or diagrams that visually represent the pattern. These charts can be particularly helpful for visual learners, as they provide a clear and concise representation of the pattern. Each symbol in the chart corresponds to a specific stitch or technique, allowing you to easily visualize the pattern and track your progress.

When reading knitting patterns, it's crucial to pay attention to the gauge or tension specified. Gauge refers to the number of stitches and rows per inch that should be achieved in order to ensure that the finished item will have the correct measurements. To achieve the correct gauge, it's important to use the recommended yarn and needle size, and to knit a swatch before starting the project. This will help you determine if you need to adjust your tension or needle size to match the pattern's gauge.

Furthermore, knitting patterns often include sizing information, which indicates the measurements for different sizes of the finished item. It's important to choose the appropriate size based on your own measurements or the intended recipient's measurements. This will ensure that the finished item fits properly and looks as intended.

In addition to the technical aspects, knitting patterns also provide guidance on the construction of the item. They typically outline the order in which the different sections of the item should be knitted, as well as any shaping or finishing techniques required. By following these instructions, you'll be able to create a well-structured and professionally finished knitted item.

Overall, understanding knitting patterns and instructions is crucial for successfully completing a knitting project. By familiarizing yourself with the abbreviations, symbols, gauge, sizing information, and construction details provided in the pattern, you'll be able to confidently tackle any knitting project and create beautiful and

Organizing Your Yarn, Needles, and Accessories of Knitting:

A Comprehensive Guide

Knitting is a beloved craft that brings joy and relaxation to many individuals. However, as any avid knitter knows, keeping your yarn, needles, and accessories organized can be quite a challenge. The last thing you want is to spend precious knitting time searching for a specific skein of yarn or a particular needle size. That's why it's essential to establish an efficient and practical organization system for your knitting supplies.

First and foremost, let's tackle the issue of yarn organization. Yarn comes in various colors, weights, and fiber types, making it crucial to have a system that allows you to easily locate the yarn you need for your projects. One popular method is to sort your yarn by color, either by using clear plastic bins or by arranging them on shelves. This method not only adds a visually appealing touch to your knitting space but also allows you to quickly identify the color you're looking for. Additionally, consider labeling your yarn bins or shelves with the specific yarn weight or fiber type, such as worsted weight or merino wool, to further streamline your search process.

Next, let's move on to needle organization. Knitting needles come in various lengths, materials, and sizes, making it essential to have a system that keeps them easily accessible and well-organized. One effective method is to use a needle case or roll-up organizer. These cases typically have individual slots or pockets for each needle size, allowing you to neatly store and protect your needles. Another option is to use a pegboard or wall-mounted organizer, where you can hang your needles by size or type. Whichever method you choose, make sure to label each slot or hook with the corresponding needle size to avoid any confusion.

Now, let's not forget about the numerous accessories that come along with knitting. Stitch markers, tapestry needles, scissors, and measuring tapes are just a few examples of the essential tools that can easily get misplaced if not properly organized. One practical solution is to use a small storage container or pouch specifically designated for these accessories. You can sort them by type or size, ensuring that you can easily find what you need when you need it. Additionally, consider investing in a magnetic strip or tray to keep your metal accessories, such as stitch markers and tapestry needles, in one place, preventing them from getting lost in the depths of your knitting bag.

Creating a Comfortable and Inspiring Knitting Zone: Creating a comfortable and inspiring knitting zone is essential for any knitting enthusiast. Whether you are a beginner or an experienced knitter, having a dedicated space where you can relax and let your creativity flow is crucial for enjoying this craft to the fullest.

First and foremost, it is important to choose a suitable location for your knitting zone. Ideally, this space should be quiet and free from distractions, allowing you to fully immerse yourself in your knitting projects. Consider setting up your knitting zone in a spare room, a cozy corner of your living room, or even a peaceful outdoor area if weather permits.

Once you have chosen the perfect location, it's time to focus on creating a comfortable seating area. Invest in a comfortable chair or a cozy armchair that provides adequate support for your back and arms. This will ensure that you can knit for extended periods without experiencing any discomfort or strain. Additionally, consider adding a footrest or a small ottoman to provide extra comfort and relaxation.

Lighting is another crucial aspect to consider when setting up your knitting zone. Natural light is always the best option, so try to position your knitting area near a window. This will not only provide ample lighting but also allow you to enjoy the view and feel connected to the outside world while you knit. If natural light is not sufficient, invest in a good quality task lamp that provides bright, focused light to prevent eye strain.

Organization is key when it comes to creating an inspiring knitting zone. Make sure you have ample storage space for your knitting supplies, such as yarn, needles, and patterns. Consider installing shelves, baskets, or storage bins to keep everything neatly organized and easily accessible. This will not only save you time searching for your materials but also create a visually appealing and clutter-free environment that promotes creativity.

To further enhance the ambiance of your knitting zone, consider adding some personal touches and decorations. Hang up inspiring quotes or artwork related to knitting on the walls. Display your finished projects or works in progress to serve as a reminder of your accomplishments and to keep you motivated. Adding plants or flowers can also bring a touch of nature and freshness to your knitting zone, creating a calming and inspiring atmosphere.

Lastly, don't forget to make your knitting zone a technology-free zone. Disconnecting from electronic devices and social media can help you fully immerse yourself in the knitting process and find a sense of peace and relaxation. Instead, consider playing soft music or audiobooks in the background to create a soothing and enjoyable knitting experience.

Starting a Knitting Journal for Your Projects: Starting a knitting journal for your projects can be a great way to keep track of your progress, document your patterns and techniques, and create a personal record of your knitting journey. Whether you are a beginner or an experienced knitter, a knitting journal can serve as a valuable tool to enhance your knitting experience.

Firstly, a knitting journal allows you to keep track of your projects in an organized manner. You can record important details such as the date you started and finished a project, the yarn and needle sizes used, and any modifications or adjustments you made to the pattern. This information can be extremely helpful when you want to recreate a project or refer back to it in the future. It also helps you to identify patterns or techniques that you particularly enjoyed or struggled with, allowing you to learn and grow as a knitter.

Additionally, a knitting journal provides a space for you to document your thoughts and experiences while working on a project. You can write about the inspiration behind the project, the challenges you faced, and the satisfaction you felt upon completing it. This personal touch adds a sentimental value to your knitting journal, making it more than just a record of patterns and techniques. It becomes a reflection of your creativity, dedication, and passion for knitting.

Furthermore, a knitting journal can serve as a source of inspiration for future projects. By flipping through the pages of your journal, you can revisit past projects and draw inspiration from the color combinations, stitch patterns, and overall designs. You may discover new ideas or find ways to improve upon previous projects. This creative aspect of a knitting journal allows you to constantly evolve and explore new possibilities in your knitting endeavors.

In addition to documenting your own projects, a knitting journal can also be a platform to connect with other knitters. You can share your journal entries, patterns, and techniques with fellow knitters through social media platforms or knitting communities. This not only allows you to receive feedback and advice, but also fosters a sense of community and camaraderie among knitters. You can learn from others, exchange ideas, and be inspired by their work, creating a supportive network of like-minded individuals.

To start a knitting journal, you can use a notebook or a dedicated journal specifically designed for knitting. You can divide it into sections for different projects, include pockets to store yarn labels or swatches, and even add photographs or sketches of your projects. The key is to make it a personalized space that reflects your own knitting style and preferences.

Understanding Design Elements in Knitting: Design elements in knitting refer to the various techniques and components that are used to create visually appealing and aesthetically pleasing knitted items. These elements include color, texture, pattern, and shape, among others. Understanding these design elements is crucial for knitters who want to create unique and beautiful pieces.

One of the most important design elements in knitting is color. The choice of colors can greatly impact the overall look and feel of a knitted item. Knitters can choose to work with a single color or multiple colors, and they can create different effects by using contrasting or complementary colors. Color can be used to highlight certain areas of a design, create visual interest, or evoke a particular mood or theme.

Texture is another key design element in knitting. Different stitch patterns and techniques can be used to create a variety of textures, from smooth and sleek to chunky and textured. Texture can add depth and dimension to a knitted item, making it more visually interesting and tactile. Knitters can experiment with different stitch patterns, such as cables, lace, or bobbles, to create unique textures and effects.

Pattern is another design element that plays a significant role in knitting. Knitting patterns can range from simple and repetitive to complex and intricate. Patterns can be created using a combination of different stitches and techniques, and they can be used to create motifs, images, or geometric designs. Knitters can follow existing patterns or create their own, allowing for endless possibilities and creativity.

Shape is also an important design element in knitting. Knitters can create different shapes by increasing or decreasing stitches, shaping with short rows, or using different construction techniques. The shape of a knitted item can greatly impact its overall look and fit. Knitters can create garments with a tailored and fitted silhouette or opt for a more relaxed and oversized shape. The choice of shape can also be influenced by the intended use of the knitted item, such as a hat, scarf, or sweater.

In addition to these design elements, other factors such as yarn choice, gauge, and finishing techniques also contribute to the overall design of a knitted item. The type of yarn used can affect the drape, texture, and appearance of the finished piece. Gauge, or the number of stitches and rows per inch, determines the size and fit of the knitted item. Finishing techniques, such as blocking, seaming, and adding embellishments, can enhance the overall look and polish of a knitted item.

Tips for Writing and Sharing Patterns of Knitting:

Writing and sharing knitting patterns can be a rewarding experience for both the pattern creator and the knitting community. Whether you are an experienced knitter looking to share your designs or a beginner wanting to document your favorite patterns, there are several tips to keep in mind to ensure your patterns are clear, concise, and enjoyable for others to follow.

1. Start with a clear and concise title: A good pattern title should accurately describe the item being knitted and give potential knitters an idea of what to expect. Avoid using vague or misleading titles that may confuse or mislead knitters.

2. Provide a detailed materials list: Include a comprehensive list of all the materials needed to complete the project, including the type and weight of yarn, needle size, and any additional tools or notions required. This will help knitters gather all the necessary supplies before starting.

3. Write clear and easy-to-follow instructions: Break down the pattern into clear and concise steps, using simple language that is easy for knitters of all skill levels to understand. Use bullet points or numbered lists to organize the instructions and make them easier to follow.

4. Include stitch abbreviations and explanations: Knitting patterns often use abbreviations for common stitches, so it's important to include a key or legend that explains each abbreviation used in the pattern. This will help knitters understand the instructions and avoid confusion.

5. Provide gauge information: Gauge refers to the number of stitches and rows per inch in a knitted fabric. Including gauge information in your pattern will help knitters ensure their finished project matches the intended size and fit. Be sure to include instructions on how to measure gauge accurately.

6. Include clear and detailed diagrams or charts: Visual aids such as diagrams or charts can greatly enhance the clarity of your pattern. Use these tools to illustrate stitch patterns, shaping instructions, or any other complex elements of the design. Make sure the diagrams are clear and easy to read.

7. Test your pattern: Before sharing your pattern with others, it's important to knit the item yourself and follow the instructions step by step. This will help you identify any errors or confusing sections that may need clarification. Consider having other knitters test your pattern as well to ensure its accuracy and clarity.

8. Use high-quality photographs: Including clear and well-lit photographs of the finished item can help knitters visualize the end result and make them more excited to start the project.

Combining Different Textures and Colors in Projects of Knitting: Combining different textures and colors in knitting projects can add depth, interest, and visual appeal to your creations. By incorporating a variety of textures and colors, you can create unique and eye-catching pieces that stand out from the crowd.

One way to incorporate different textures in your knitting projects is by using a combination of yarns with varying thicknesses. For example, you can pair a chunky yarn with a finer yarn to create a contrasting texture. This can be particularly effective when knitting accessories such as scarves or hats, as the different textures will add dimension and visual interest to the finished piece.

Another way to add texture to your knitting projects is by incorporating different stitch patterns. By alternating between simple and more complex stitch patterns, you can create a visually dynamic piece. For example, you can combine a basic stockinette stitch with a more intricate cable or lace pattern. This combination of textures will not only add visual interest but also create a tactile experience for the wearer.

In addition to textures, incorporating different colors into your knitting projects can also enhance their overall aesthetic. Color can be used to create contrast, highlight certain elements, or evoke a specific mood. For example, pairing complementary colors such as blue and orange can create a vibrant and energetic look, while using analogous colors such as green and yellow can create a harmonious and calming effect.

When combining different colors in your knitting projects, it's important to consider the overall color scheme and balance. You can choose to use a monochromatic color scheme, where different shades of the same color are used, or opt for a more contrasting color scheme by combining complementary or contrasting colors. Experimenting with different color combinations can help you discover unique and visually appealing results.

Furthermore, incorporating different textures and colors in your knitting projects allows you to personalize and customize your creations. Whether you're knitting a sweater, a blanket, or a pair of socks, adding a variety of textures and colors can make your project truly one-of-a-kind. It allows you to express your creativity and showcase your individual style.

In conclusion, combining different textures and colors in knitting projects can elevate your creations to new heights. By incorporating a variety of yarn thicknesses, stitch patterns, and color schemes, you can create visually dynamic and unique pieces that are sure to impress. So, don't be afraid to experiment and let your creativity shine through in your knitting projects.

Introduction

Knitting is making a comeback these days with people looking for DIY activities, non-electronic hobbies, and ways to de-stress.

For multitaskers, what better way is there to keep your hands busy, make something, and be able to watch videos or chat with friends simultaneously? Of course, you don't have to do all those things at once if you don't want to!

Let's concentrate on knitting quick and handy projects for items you can wear, use yourself, or give as gifts.

This book describes ways to make simple knitting projects that appeal to all ages, especially tweens and teens - as I discovered with my daughters and their friends.

If you've already mastered the basic techniques of knitting (i.e., the knit stitch, the purl stitch, casting on, and casting off), then you are more than ready to tackle the projects described in this book.

These projects include:

> A pair of multi-colored hand warmers
> A phone cozy
> An infinity scarf
> A braided headband

With each of these projects, you'll build on your basic knitting knowledge. You will learn simple new techniques that make your finished product look advanced but actually are easy to execute.

Variety is the spice of life, and you'll be working with different weights of yarn and types of needles as well!

Any time you are unsure of a knitting term or technique, look it up on the internet: knitting websites and YouTube demonstrations can be incredibly helpful resources.

Don't be intimidated—all of these projects provide endless, effortless fun. Are you ready?

Chapter 1: Multicolored Hand Warmers

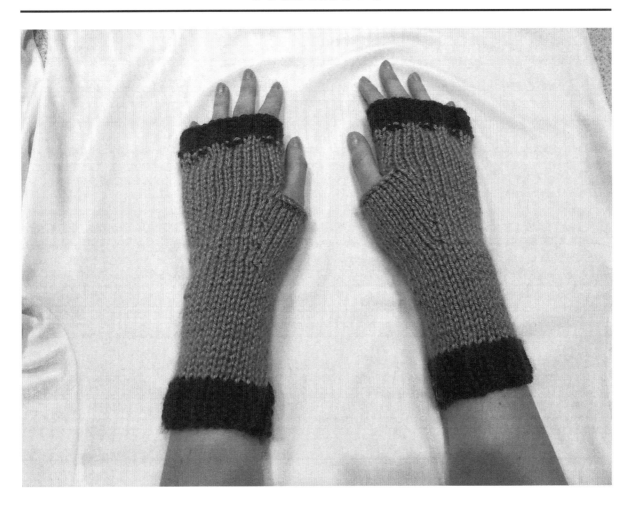

Do your hands ever feel slightly cold? Chilly enough for a little covering but not enough to pull on full gloves or thick mittens?

If so, try making these popular hand warmers. Cozy and convenient, they keep hands toasty while leaving fingers free to move and complete tasks unencumbered.

Get things done without sacrificing comfort! These hand warmers are perfect to wear while texting on the phone, typing at the computer, holding a book and turning pages while reading, practicing the piano, taking ballet class, etc.

With this project, you'll learn how to change yarn colors, execute a Make One (M1) stitch, and cast on stitches in the middle of a row.

Gather the following supplies:

> one skein (at most 5 ounces, 251 yards) of medium worsted weight (4) yarn in Color A for the piece's body. Acrylic, acrylic-wool blend, or wool is fine.
> a half skein of medium worsted weight (4) yarn in Color B (contrasting color) for the piece's ribbing
> one pair of size 8 straight knitting needles
> two stitch markers
> one tapestry needle
> row counter (optional)

This one-size-fits-all pattern is suitable for the average teen/adult. Feel free to adjust it (length-wise, width-wise) if you wish.

Each hand warmer's finished circumference at the upper and lower edges is about seven inches. The finished length from the top edge to the bottom edge is about nine and a half inches.

Be sure to check your gauge. The gauge for this pattern is 18 stitches by 16 rows equaling about four square inches in stockinette stitch.

If you end up needing to knit fewer stitches and rows to make a four-inch square, try using smaller size needles. If you end up needing to knit more stitches and rows to make a four-inch square, try using a larger size needle

This pattern can be used for both the left-hand and right-hand fingerless mittens. However, if you want the side seam to be positioned under each hand when you wear the finished mitten, then use these directions for the hand/thumb gusset section of the left-hand warmer:

Step 1: Cast on 28 stitches in Color B.

Step 2: Create the bottom ribbing by working in K2, P2 (rib stitch) for 6 rows (about one inch).

Step 3: Change Yarn Colors: change to Color A yarn.

Hold the finished ribbing as if you are going to knit your next row.

Instead of continuing to use Color B yarn, however, take Color A yarn and wrap it around the right needle a few times to prevent it from slipping off easily.

Start knitting with the right needle but use Color A yarn, not Color B yarn.

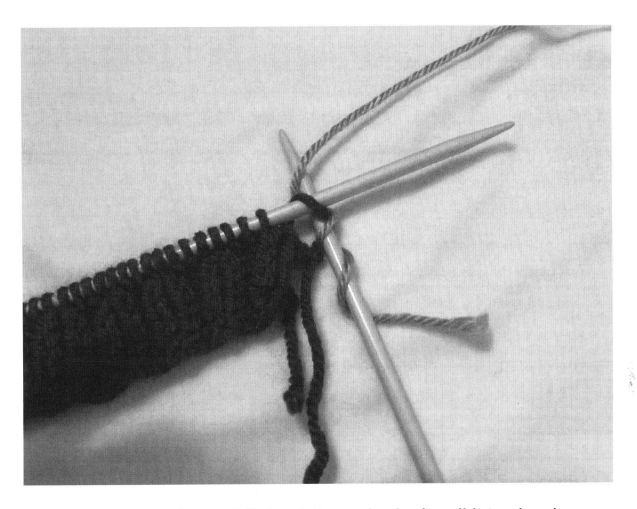

As you pull the loop of Color A through, don't pull it too hard as you may end up pulling Color A yarn off the right needle.

Tip: Hold onto the "tails" of both Colors A and B as while knitting the first few stitches in Color A.

Complete the first knit stitch in Color A–it becomes the first stitch on the right needle.

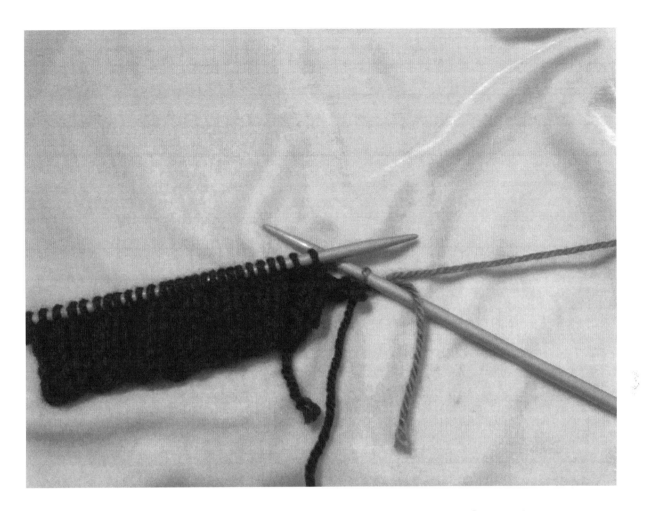

Repeat steps 2 and 3 to knit the second stitch in Color A.

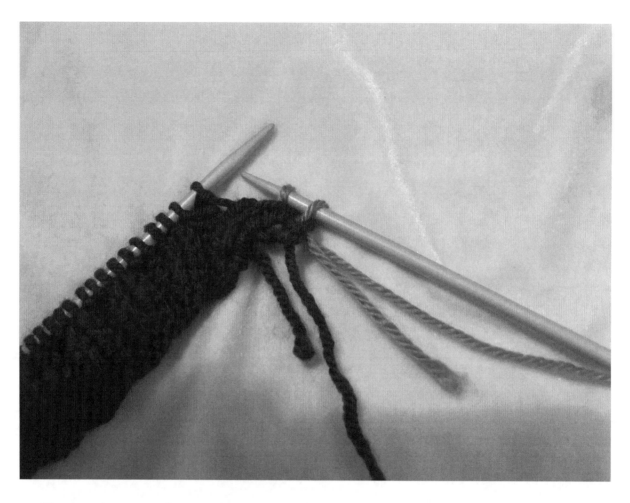

Repeat steps 2 and 3 to knit a few more stitches. Tie the "tails" of Colors A and B into a knot to anchor Color A.

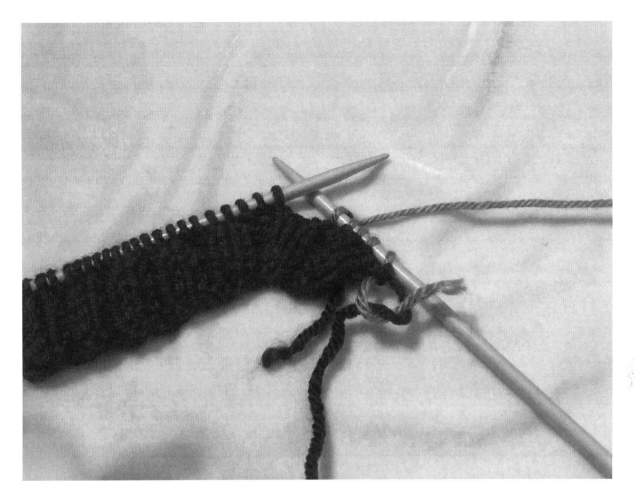

Cut the "tail" of Color B to free it from its skein; you are now working from the skein of Color A.

Step 4: Finish knitting the row in Color A and enjoy the contrasting colors!

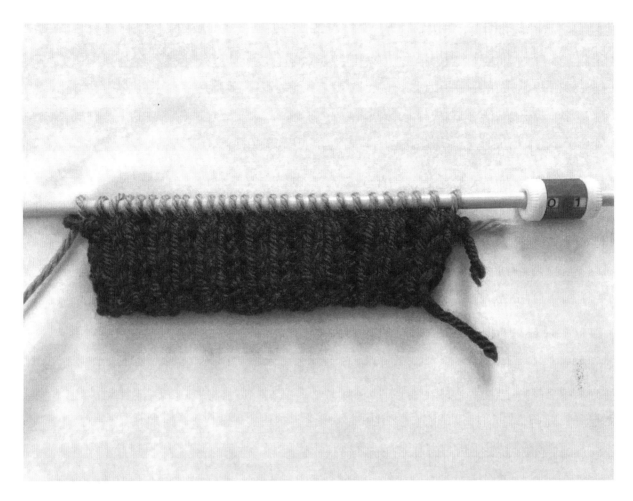

Step 5: Then create the hand warmer's lower half, the section that covers the wrist by working in stockinette stitch for about three inches (another 17 rows).

Step 6: Now, you're ready to create the hand/thumb gusset section.

<u>Row 1</u>: K1, PM (place a marker on the needle). This is the mitten's right side (RS: knit/out-facing).

Execute M1 (make one stitch)

Add or increase by one knit stitch by lifting the horizontal thread lying between needles from the back with the right needle.

Then place the stitch onto the left needle and use the right needle to knit a new stitch through the back loop.

Voil à –you have made (added/increased by) one new stitch on the right needle, just left of the marker.

Then K6, M1, and PM (place the second marker on the needle).

Then knit to the end of the row. You've now increased or added two new stitches.

Rows 2-4: Continue in stockinette stitch.

Row 5: K1, slip marker (SM), M1, knit to next marker, M1, SM, knit to the end of the row. You've increased or added two new stitches.

Rows 6-8: Continue in stockinette stitch.

Row 9: repeat Row 5. You've increased or added two new stitches.

Rows 10-12: Continue in stockinette stitch.

Row 13: repeat Row 5. You've increased or added two new stitches.

Row 14: Purl to marker, remove marker, P2, bind off 10 stitches for thumb opening, P2, remove marker, and purl to end of row.

<u>Row 15</u>: Knit to the bound-off stitches.

Cast On in the Middle of This Row: here are instructions for how to cast on 2 stitches over the bound-off stitches.

Turn over the work, so the purl side (wrong side: WS) is facing up.

Bring yarn between needles to back.

Insert right needle through the front (from left to right) of the end stitch on the left needle.

Wind the yarn around, behind, and then over the right needle.

Use the right needle to pull through the loop.

Use the right needle to pull the loop off the left needle but keep the end stitch on the left needle.

Insert the left needle under the loop (from right front) on the right needle.

Slide the left needle through the loop, remove the right needle from the loop and voil à - you've cast on 1 stitch in the middle of a row.

Repeat the above steps in order to cast on the second stitch in the middle of this row.

Then turn the work back over again, so RS is facing up.

Continue to knit to the end of the row, closing the hole you've just created for the thumb.

Knit to the end of this row.

Step 7: Knit in stockinette stitch for about one and a half inches (9 rows).

Step 8: To create the top ribbing, change back to yarn Color B and K2, P2 (rib stitch) for the next 6 rows, about one inch.

Step 5: Cast off stitches loosely in rib stitch.

For the hand/thumb gusset section of the *right*-hand warmer:

Step 1: Cast on 28 stitches in Color B.

Step 2: Create the bottom ribbing by working in K2, P2 (rib stitch) for 6 rows (about one inch).

Step 3: Change to Color A yarn and knit 1 row.

Continue creating the hand warmer's lower half (i.e., the section that covers the wrist) by working in stockinette stitch for about three inches (another 17 rows).

Step 4: Create the hand/thumb gusset section.

<u>Row 1</u>: K21, PM, M1, K6, M1, PM, K1.

Since the beginning, you have increased or added two new stitches, bringing the total number of stitches in this row to 30.

<u>Rows 2-4</u>: Continue in stockinette stitch.

<u>Row 5</u>: K1 to marker, SM, M1, knit to next marker, M1, SM, knit to the end of the row. You've increased or added two new stitches.

<u>Rows 6-8</u>: Continue in stockinette stitch.

<u>Row 9</u>: repeat Row 5. You've increased or added two new stitches.

<u>Rows 10-12</u>: Continue in stockinette stitch.

Row 13: repeat Row 5. You've increased or added two new stitches.

Row 14: (WS) Purl to marker, remove marker, P2, bind off 10 stitches for thumb opening, P2, remove marker, and purl to end of row.

Row 15: (RS) Knit, casting on 2 stitches over bound-off stitches. You've increased or added two new stitches.

Step 5: Knit in stockinette stitch for about one and a half inches (9 rows).

Step 6: To create the top ribbing, change back to Color B yarn and K2, P2 (rib stitch) for the next 6 rows, about one inch.

Step 7: Cast off stitches loosely in rib stitch. Now you have finished hand warmer pieces.

Step 8: Fold the finished piece in half lengthwise, wrong side to the wrong side. Use a tapestry needle to sew the side seam.

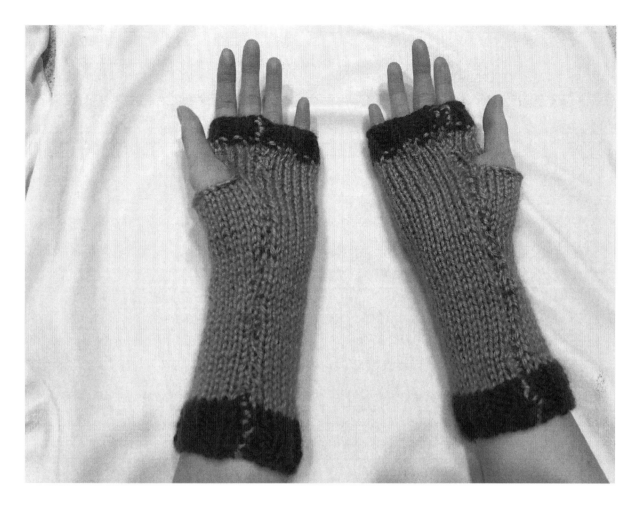

Customize the hand warmers as you wish.

You may lengthen the wrist section for more coverage, shorten the wrist section for less coverage, cast on more stitches to widen, or fewer stitches to make narrower in multiples of four.

All the while, still follow the basic pattern shape.

In this next chapter, we'll create a cover for your phone.

Chapter 2: Basket Weave Phone Cozy

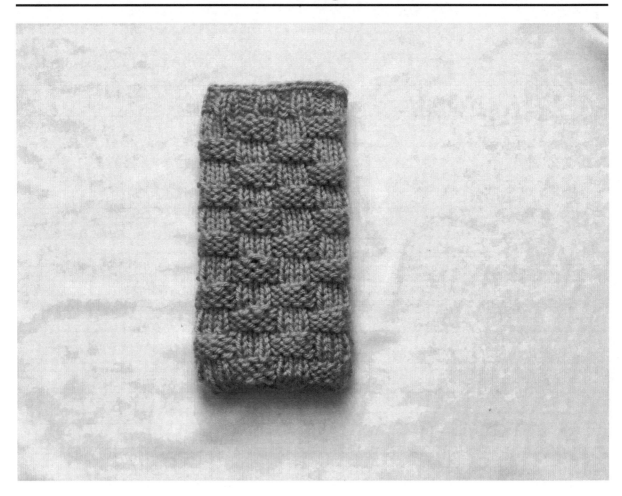

Since nearly everyone has a cell phone nowadays, this practical and quick project can be used by anyone.

Although many people protect their cell phones with cases, this basket weave phone cozy adds a soft touch and can prevent screens and cases (or naked phones) from getting scratched.

Here's an idea: actually put your phone away, but not too far away or buried in a bag.

Put it in the basket weave phone cozy to keep it from becoming a distraction while still easily accessible.

With this project, you'll learn how to use double pointed needles (DPN) to knit in the round and to join end stitches in the round.

Gather the following supplies:

10g of double knitting (DK)/lightweight (3) yarn
four size 6 (4mm) double pointed needles
one stitch marker
one tapestry needle
needle point protectors/stoppers (optional)
row counter (optional)

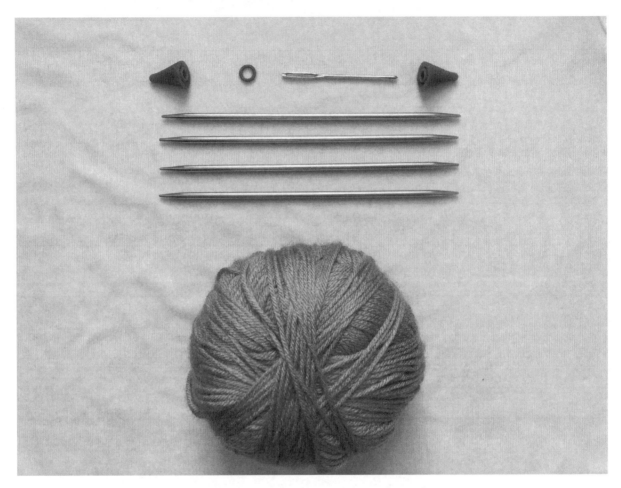

DPN are often used for knitting in the round for seamless cylindrical items with small circumferences and diameters, such as socks or leg warmers.

Working with DPN isn't difficult, but because both ends of each are pointed, stitches can slip off easily. Therefore, knitters new to DPN might want to try DPN made from wood, which are less slippery than metal or plastic needles.

Needle point protectors—which look like mini rubber cones—are meant to protect the ends of needles, keep them sharp, and prevent them from poking other objects.

They also stop stitches from sliding off (which protects my sanity, keeps me happy, and prevents me from stabbing other objects in frustration).

Although gauge is important is most knitting projects, it isn't really crucial for this project. This pattern can fit loosely over an iPhone 8 with a thin case or fits snugly over an iPhone 10R with an OtterBox case.

Step 1: Cast on 32 stitches on one needle.

Step 2: Transfer 22 stitches onto a second needle, slipping the stitches as if to purl.

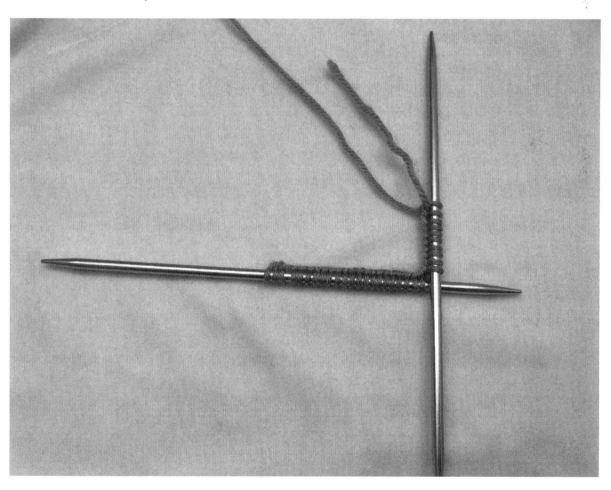

Step 3: Transfer 11 stitches from the second needle onto the third needle. Position the three needles in a U shape.

You should have 10 stitches on the first needle (right side of the U), 11 stitches on the second needle (bottom of U), and 11 stitches on the third needle (left side of the U).

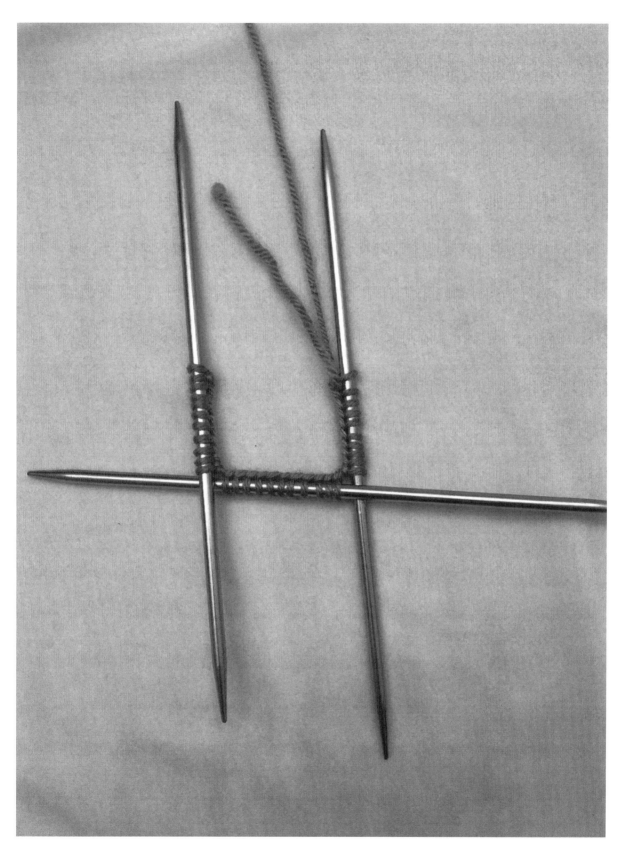

Step 4: Join end stitches in the round.

Position the three needles into a triangle.

Insert the right needle in front of and under the end stitch on the left needle.

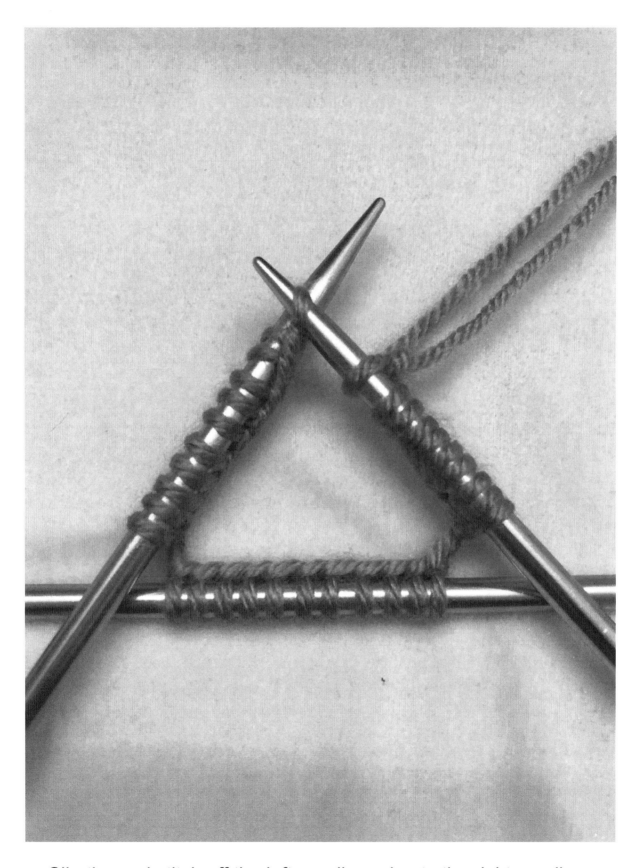

Slip the end stitch off the left needle and onto the right needle.

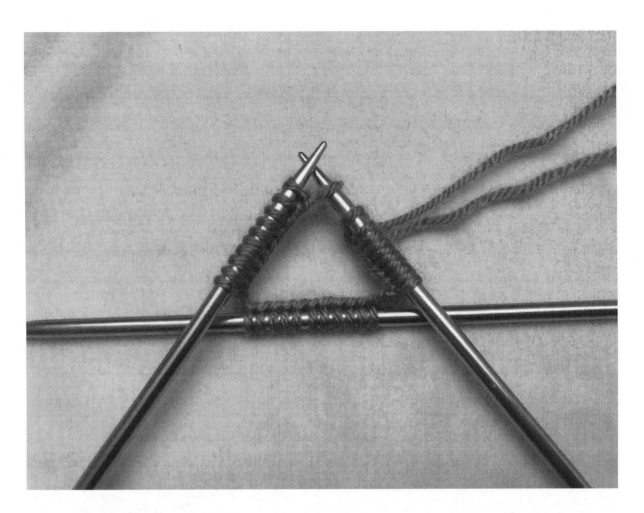

Insert the left needle in front of and under the next-to-end stitch
(what used to be the end stitch) on the right needle.

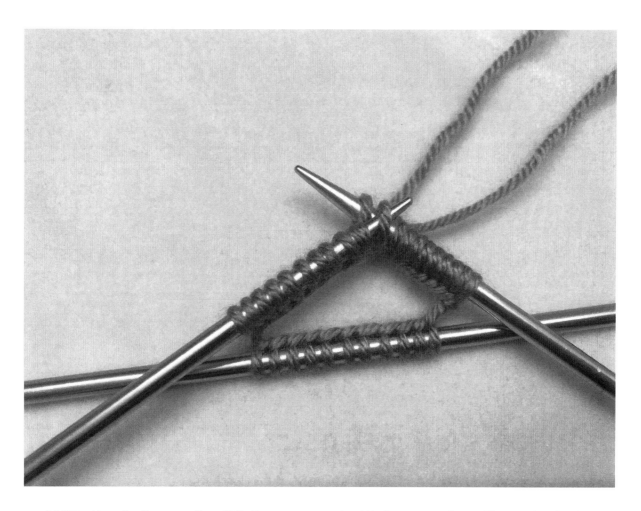

With the left needle, lift the second stitch over the slipped stitch and off the right needle; now the stitch is on the left needle.

The two slipped stitches should cross each other.

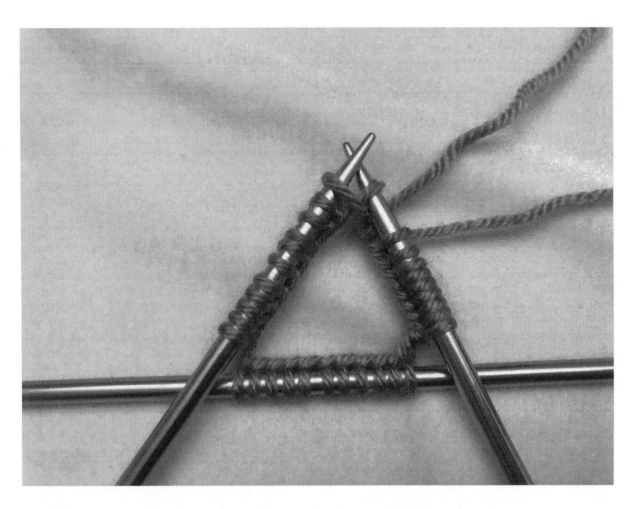

Step 5: Use the fourth DPN to begin knitting in the round.

At the beginning of a round (row), knit 1 stitch, PM, and then knit the rest of the row.

Once you've completed one row, you'll know that your next row begins when there is one stitch left before the stitch marker.

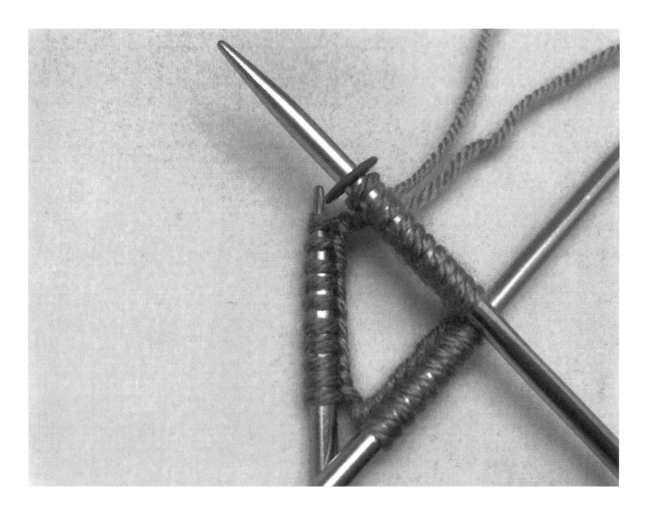

As you knit, you'll be transferring stitches from one needle to another, thus freeing up one needle each time you finish one needle.

Use the free needle to knit the next needle.

Tip: If you want to use a counter to keep track of what row you are on, put a round counter on the end of one of the needles, or use a hand counter.

Step 6: Follow this pattern.

<u>Row 1</u>: Knit

<u>Row 2:</u> (P5, K3) four times

Row 3: (P5, K3) four times

Row 4: (P5, K3) four times

Row 5: Knit

Row 6: (P1, K3, P5, K3, P4) two times

Row 7: (P1, K3, P5, K3, P4) two times

Row 8: (P1, K3, P5, K3, P4) two times

Step 7: Repeat Rows 1 through 8 five more times or until the case fits over your phone with an inch to go.

Step 8: End in a knit row.

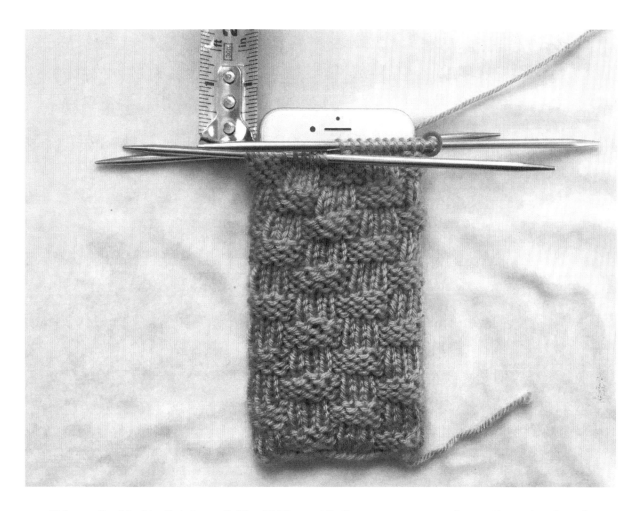

Step 9: Knit ribbing (K2, P2) until the case reaches the desired length past the end of your phone.

Step 10: Cast off stitches loosely in rib stitch.

Step 11: Use a tapestry needle to sew the bottom seam of the phone case.

Chapter 3: Double Moss Infinity Scarf

Infinity scarves are all the rage. They're stylish, convenient, and easy to wear without any ends to tuck in.

Infinity scarves look great on anyone at any age, but I noticed my daughters and friends knitting them quite often as their project of choice.

With this double moss infinity scarf project, you'll learn how to use a circular needle to knit in the round, join end stitches in the round, and knit the double moss stitch pattern.

Gather the following supplies:

    three skeins of bulky weight (5) yarn (about 300-400 yards)
    US 13 (9 mm) 29" circular needle
    one stitch marker
    row counter (optional)

As with DPN, circular needles are used for knitting in the round.

Unlike DPN, though, circular needles are one single neat piece: two needles joined by a cord for holding stitches.

Also, stitches are not as likely to easily slip off circular needles.

Finally, while DPN are used for knitting small circular items (like socks), circular needles can accommodate larger projects.

Circular needles come in varying lengths, from nine inches (for baby hats) to 40+ inches (for larger flat projects like bed-size blankets).

Although gauge is important is most knitting projects, it isn't really as crucial for this project because this scarf is not anywhere near form-fitting.

A finished double moss infinity scarf measures about 11 inches wide with a circumference of 78 inches.

Step 1: Cast on 134 stitches.

Step 2: Join end stitches in the round.

Insert the right needle under end stitch on the left needle.

Slip end stitch off the left needle and onto the right needle.

Insert the left needle in front of and under the next-to-end stitch (what used to be the end stitch) on the right needle.

With the left needle, lift the second stitch over the slipped stitch and off the right needle; now the stitch is on the left needle.

The two slipped stitches should cross each other.

Step 3: Knit 1 stitch, place stitch marker (PM), and then knit the rest of the round (row).

Once you've completed one row, you'll know that your next row begins when there is one stitch left before the stitch marker.

Tip: If you want to use a counter to keep track of what row you are on, hang a counter from the stitch marker, or use a hand counter.

Step 4: Begin knitting pattern in the round.

Row 1: K2, P2 (repeat to end of the row)

<u>Row 2</u>: P2, K2 (repeat to end of the row)

The resulting pattern is a double moss stitch.

Step 5: Work until piece measures about 11 inches wide or as wide as you wish.

Step 6: Bind off loosely.

Wearing this double moss stitch infinity scarf in style is easy. Loop it around your neck and straighten it out full length.

Twist it to make a second loop.

Pull the second loop over your head.

Chapter 4: Braided Cable Headband

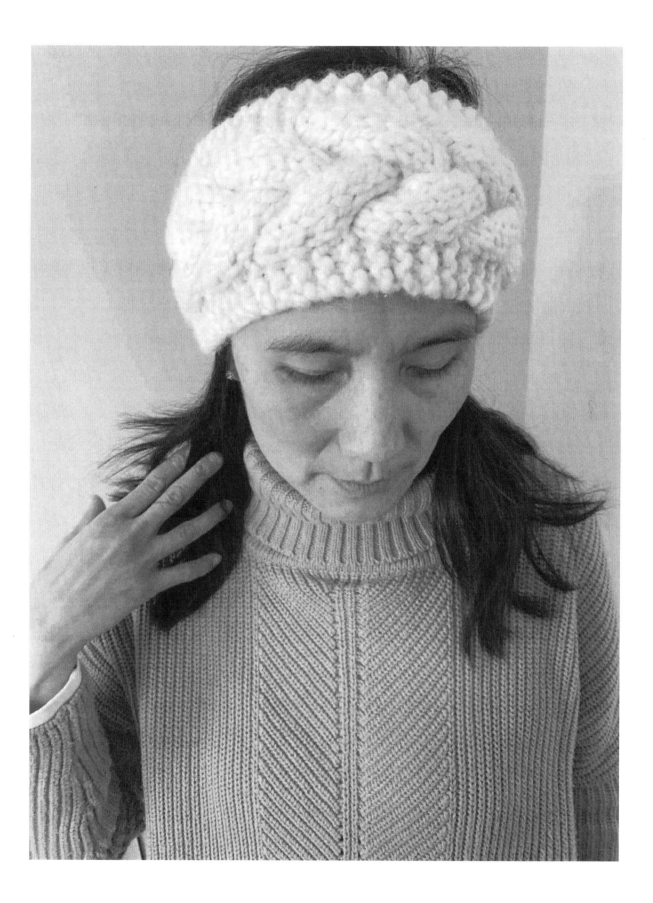

Need to keep your head warm but don't want to wear a hat? Want a more stylish look than ear muffs?

Then try making and wearing this braided cable headband.

With this project, you'll learn how to knit a braided cable, which looks fancy but is pretty easy.

Gather the following supplies:

one skein (about 100 grams, 87 yards) of super bulky weight (6) yarn
one pair of size 10.5 straight knitting needles
one cable needle (CN)–U-shaped (shown, but you can use another-shaped CN if you wish)
one tapestry needle
row counter

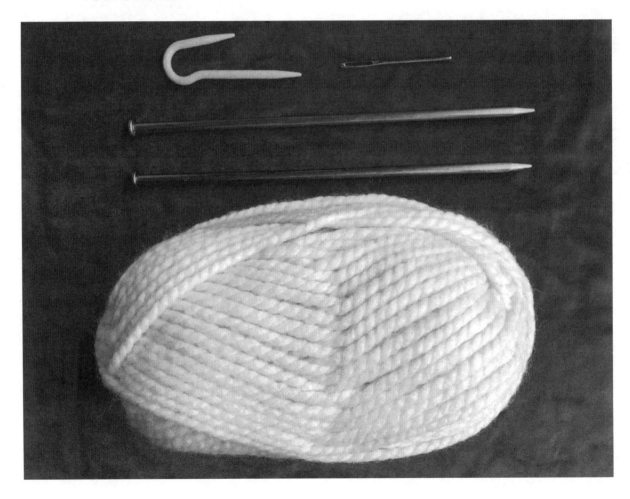

Step 1: Cast on 18 stitches.

Step 2: Follow this stitch pattern.

<u>Row 1</u>: K18

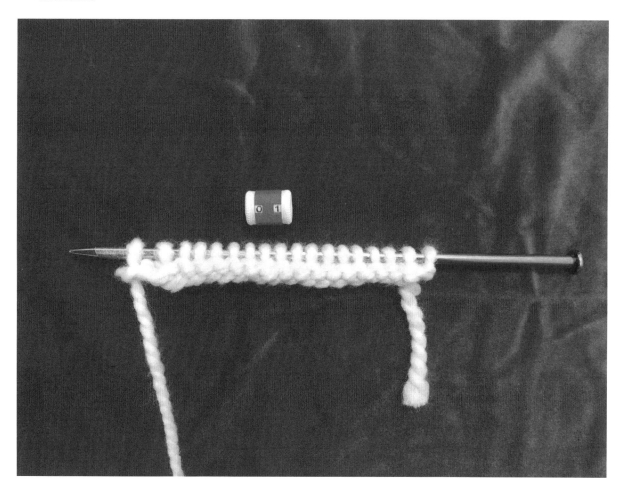

<u>Row 2</u>: K3, P12, K3

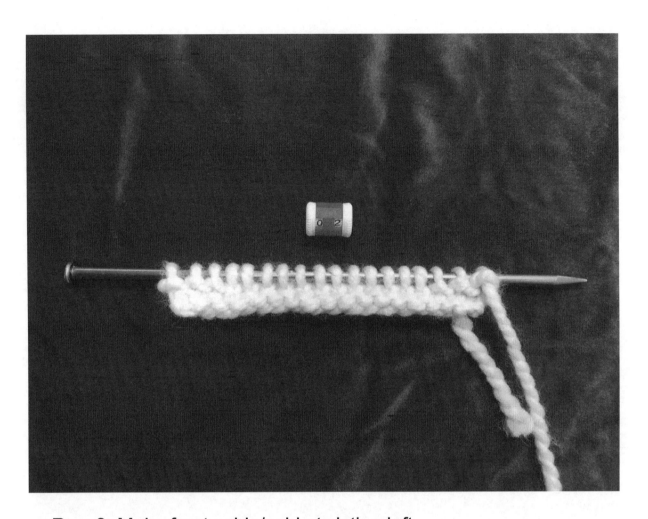

<u>Row 3</u>: Make front cable/cable twisting left.

K3, slip the next 4 stitches to the CN and hold in front

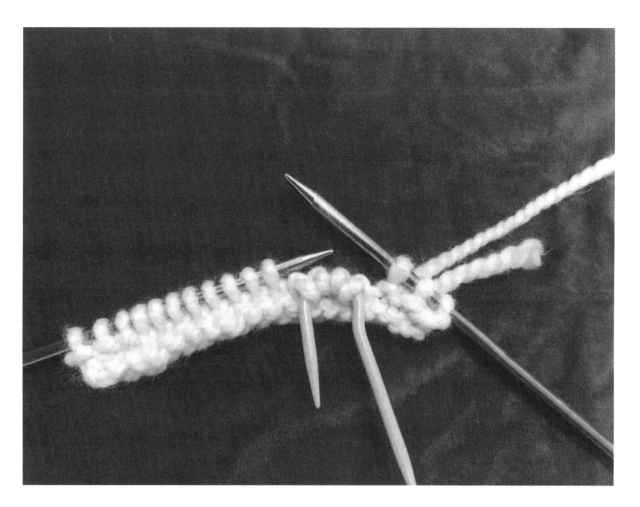

K4 from the left needle

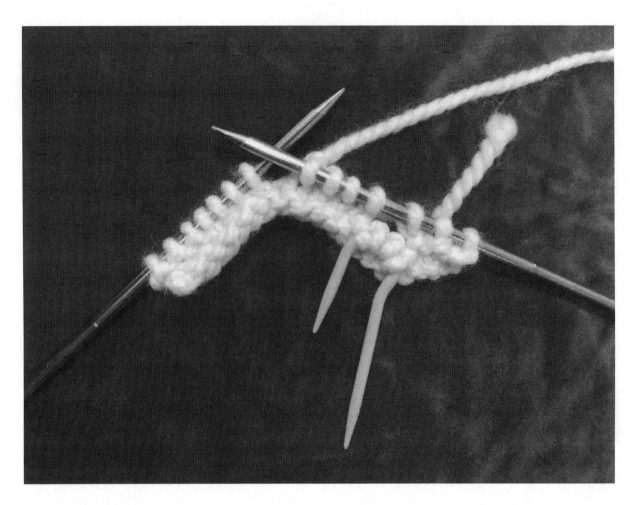

K4 from CN

K7

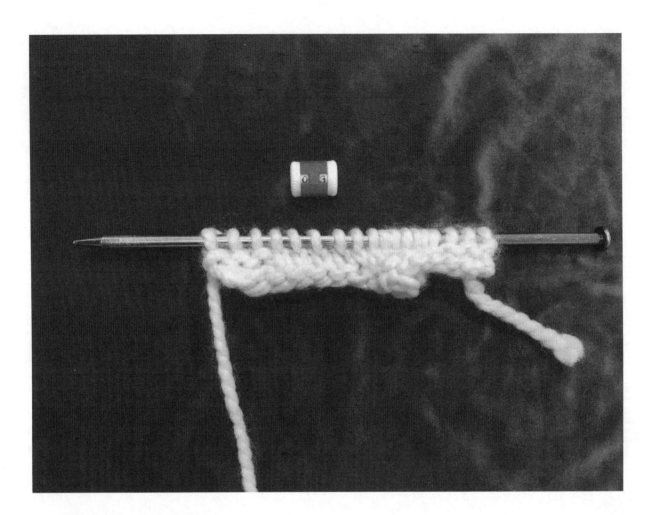

<u>Row 4</u>: K3, P12, K3

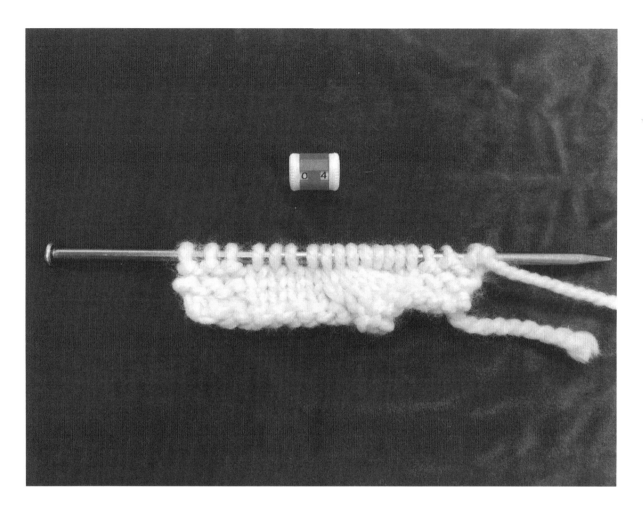

<u>Row 5</u>: K18

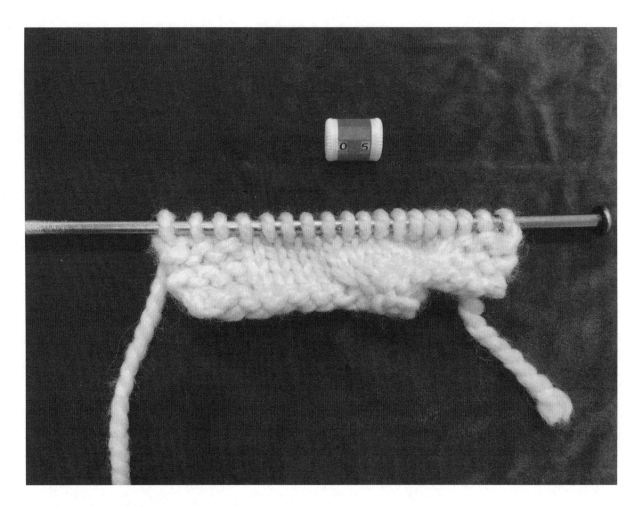

<u>Row 6</u>: K3, P12, K3

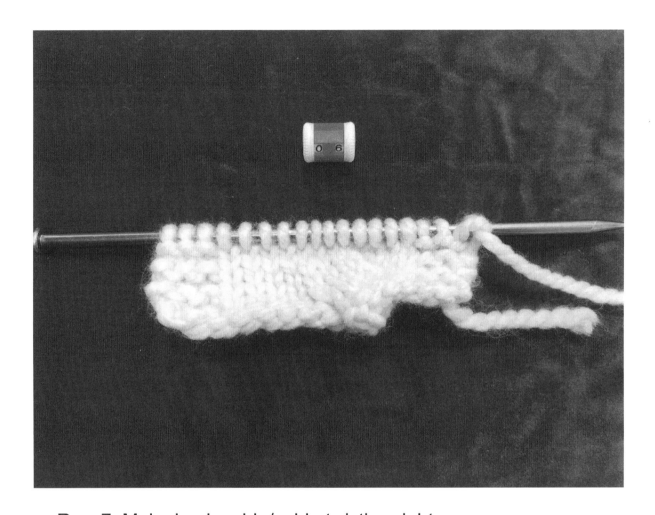

<u>Row 7</u>: Make back cable/cable twisting right.

K7, slip the next 4 stitches to the CN and hold in back

K4 from left needle

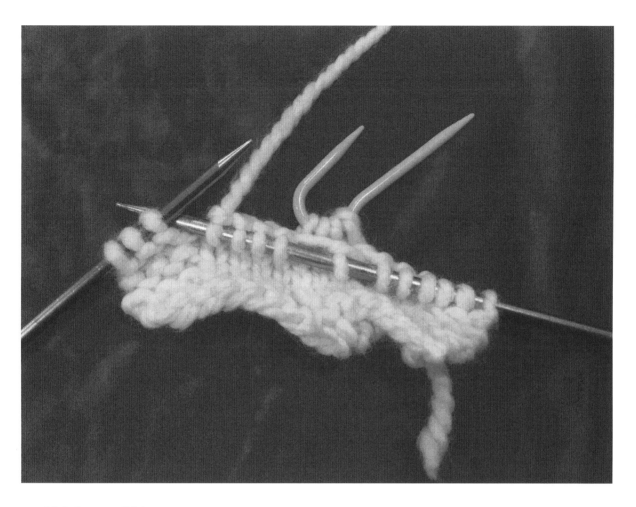

K4 from CN

K3

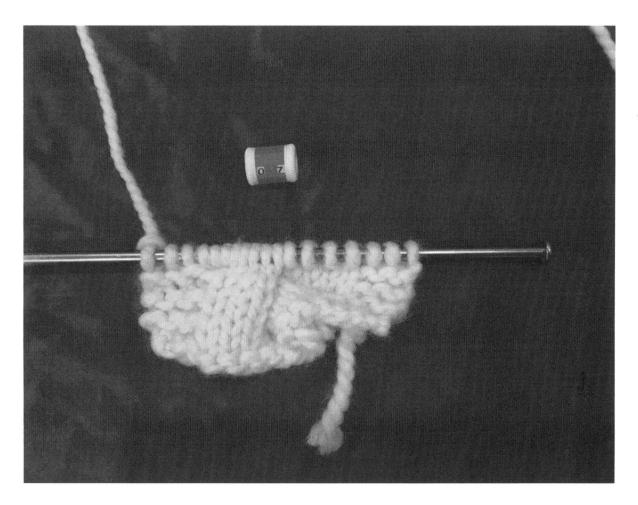

<u>Row 8</u>: K3, P12, K3

Step 3: Repeat Rows 1 through 8 eleven times or until the headband measures to the desired length.

It should be long enough to wrap around your head with a one-inch gap.

Tip: Purposely leave the headband a little short, so it is well fitted and stays on your head when you wear it; it stretches out.

Step 4: End on a row with K18, cast off loosely and sew the ends together.

Step 5: Bind off and use a tapestry needle to sew the short ends together.

Conclusion

Congratulations! Pat yourself on the back because you've graduated beyond beginner knitting!

You've added more techniques to your "knitting toolbox." Just think about all the flexibility you now have!

You have now learned these advanced knitting techniques:

Using double pointed needles (DPN) to knit in the round
How to use a circular needle to knit in the round
Using a cable needle
How to change yarn colors in the middle of a project
Increase or add a stitch through M1
Cast on stitches in the middle of a row
Knit a basket weave pattern
Knit the Double Moss Stitch pattern
Knit a braided cable
Join end stitches in the round.

On top of that, you now have experience working with different weights of yarn, including:

DK (double knitting) weight or lightweight (3)
medium worsted weight (4)
bulky weight (5)
super bulky weight (6).

Finally, don't forget that you can customize any of these projects because you decide what type of yarn you want to us, as long as it's the weight required by the project's pattern.

Browse through yarns of different colors (bright, earth tone, pastel, mixed), fibers (acrylic, wool, cotton, combinations of these), and textures (regular, fuzzy, bouclé). Play around and experiment with various types of yarn to dress up or dress down any project.

Proudly put your personal touch on anything you knit because you have the freedom, creativity, and know-how. Enjoy knitting when chilling out or on the go. In the end, you'll have a cool finished product.

If this book of projects has inspired you and helped you in any way, would you be so kind as to leave a review wherever you purchased this book? That would help me in return. Thanks for reading!

Happy knitting!

Printed in Great Britain
by Amazon

34909121R00068